GW00497041

Gill you wonderful soul,

I hope you
enjoy reading this
♡

All my love,

Janine ———— xmas
—x—— 2019

Thanks for
everything ♡

THE HYMN is a song
of spiritual awakening.

The hypnotic and iconoclastic
verse of this small talisman of a book is
published with the hope that the reader may
discover within the words their own
universal *song of the soul*.

*   *   *

A single edition of the original book exists.

Designed by the author, printed via
letterpress in New York, and hand-bound in
London, the extravagantly produced
one-of-a-kind book was a gift to the recipient
dedicated herein. This book is a
facsimile of that gift.

The original may be viewed at:

THEHYMN.COM

THE HYMN
SONG OF THE SOUL

ISBN 9780994644411

para lirio blanco

XVII

PART ONE

PRELUDE

I AM
   The One.
     All this is me.
Fathom I mislaid
   this most precious jewel,
     and forgot,
   my Soul is
     forever free—

When I think toward a time
   when I was not,
     the mind melts.
When I move within the place
   that once contained me,
     the body passes through.

My ears are all hearing,
   yet I hear silences sing in unison.
My vision is unobscured,
   still I see nothing.

Now lost in knowing,
   too wise for wisdom,
     too holy to pray.
I realize I am again
   the no-thing.

That mad, merciless
  mystery.
And finally, at once,
  the nothing
    is utterly me.

So hold my hand,
  I shall take you nowhere.
Trace my steps,
  I shall lead you toward emptiness.
Listen to my words,
  I shall speak in silence.

I sing a freedom song.
  I walk a victory march.
I dance naked,
  and enter the void.

        Follow me—

I am the heir to eternity,
  and no one shall ever know.
I am the conqueror of existence;
  I have no treasures to show.

I am the house,
  the builder of the house,
    the one who lives inside.
I am the temple,
  the pilgrim,
    the secret prayers he hides.

I need nothing;
  know nothing.

I am stillness,
  the perfect vision.
I am silence,
  the complete sound.
I am love,
  the zenith gesture.
I am forever,
  the burial ground.

Here and not here.
  There and not there.

My mythical ways
are renowned.

VERSE II

I am timeless;
   the past dies in my bosom.
I am limitless;
   the future begets from my loins.

I am the womb of the mother,
   and the seed of the father.
The babe bursts forth
   screaming my name.

I am spring who devours winter's
               ashes.
   I am summer who scorches life.
I summon the pallbearer, autumn,
   who buries the husband
      beneath the tears
of his dear,
      beloved wife.

Imagine,
   I ever tried to fill my days?
      —I am the day!
Remember,
   I once feared the night?
      —I made darkness!

I complete myself.

As prophets and devils
   waltz under constellations of past,
     I lie down,
   and I do not care.
I am divinely indifferent.
   The child of a royal family;
     spoiled
   —senseless.

I have no responsibility.
No man walks ahead of me,
   and no man chases my heels.
Charity and Piety
   slip to bed with Selfishness and
               Greed.
I undress them
   and walk away
     —I am free.

I have no respectability.
   I strip myself,
     tempt the crowds toward me.
     Bark! Like a mad dog at the wind.
When people rush to muzzle me;
   I run away,
     and spin,

and spin
   —and spin.

I have no care,
   and I do not care.
I am free;
   I am free

    —I am free.

VERSE IV

I wander where the wild winds
    of existence never blow.
I idle the dreadful deserts
      where only saints dare go.
I frequent that formidable place
      beyond the dreaded pines of
            mind.

And in those hidden haunts,
    I treasure myself.
      I entertain myself.
    I love myself,
      I hate myself,
    I slay myself,
      I ridicule myself.

I am nothing other than
    —my naked self.

Sexless,
    deathless,
      formless.
Desiring everything;
    wanting nothing.

I am God-smacked!

I art in Heaven.

Let me be,
  let me be

  —let me be.

VERSE V

You who are thunder,
   sing my loud, unchanging
             testament.
You who are lightning,
   strike my vivid, violent vision.
You who are rain,
   flood the world
     with my self-knowledge.

For I am virgin and libertine;
   madman and saint.
I am the law and the lawless one.
I am the shackled and the free.
I am the rock and the leaf.
I am the man of war;
   and she who brings peace.

I have neither disciples,
   house of worship,
     nor teaching.
I am not to be followed,
   venerated,
     or listened to.

I am the end of your world,
   and the beginning of time.

I am the end of time,
   and the beginning
      of your world.

Know the old yoke that bound me,
   lies burnt to the ground.
Born again,
   I am destined to live

     —unbound.

VERSE VI

I am a rope joined at each end;
   I go round and round.
I give birth to my lean self,
   again and again.
You may drink from my cup,
   yet I already drank you.
You may seek my land,
   yet you are already here.

When war breaks out,
   I sever my hands.
When peace prevails,
   I feed my mouth.
Why should I care for the state of
         things,
   when all this
     is ever myself?

For I am immortal.
   Unchanging,
     forged within.
Taintless, formless
   —I am the enemy of death.

I copulate with oblivions.
   I swim with leviathans.

Even nothing
    shall not stop me.

So I abide forever,
    in the ancient present.
I wait,
    for all my eternities.

Then seek no initiation
    toward my mystery.
Steer clear of those who
    dare conceal me.
I am right here,
    right now.

Learn to lose yourself

    —you will find me.

PART TWO

I am not the name forced upon me,
   the body given to me,
      or the land that claims me.
I am not my weaknesses.
I am not the age, sex,
   creed, or color
      that I landed in.

I am not the tasks asked of me,
   nor the gold paid to me.
I am not a ballot vote.
   I swear no sacred oath.
I care not what the masses say.
   I fear no final judgment day.
These games are all yours,
   and gladly
      I leave you to your shadow play.

Welcoming everything.
   Rejecting nothing.
I let go of attachment;
   I invite disaster.
The neighbors throw on the locks
   when they hear me coming.
Then, at midnight,
   I sneak into their houses

                    nevertheless,
            and plant apple trees
        while they sleep.

When adults see me,
        they cross the street.
When children find me,
        they chase my heels.
When the storm rolls in,
        the jungle curls at my feet
                for protection.

Behold me—
        Hold me—
                Holy me!
        Holy! Holy! Holy!

I am a miracle
        before my very own eyes.
I run my hands
        over my ready, pink lips.
I squeeze myself
        into this bloody bone sack of skin.

I lure my One-Mind

        —back within.

VERSE VIII

I know of fear,
   but his shadow no longer haunts
         me.
I know of regret,
   yet her memory lies behind me.
I know of pain,
   and these wounds shall not scar
         me.
I know of loss,
   still I have let my child go.
All these things,
   and many more I have,
      though they do not have me.

I am bound to no heart.
   I tend the feet of no idols.
Being unborn,
   I am exempt from old age.
I do not lay plans
   for times not come to pass.
I do not dig up my wisdom
   from the past.
I am naturalness.
   Superb—
      naturalness.

Then, daring deeply,
   you shall find me.
Never looking within,
   you shall go without me.
Forgetting me,
   you shall lose yourself.
Forgetting yourself,
   you shall find me.

Indeed
   my soil works
      in extraordinary ways.

I move as easy as the wind blows.
   My dreams spiral out
      like the conch shells.

My language is silence.
   My land is right here.
      My time is forever.

My lesson is
   just this
      —Now.

VERSE IX

Like finding the snowflake
  upon the mountain
    —I defy you.
Like following a raindrop
  through the ocean
    —I escape you.

Know this is my home,
  understand you never left.
And though we shared the world
        together,
  And though we trod a life
        together;
  I do not miss you
  —I am you.

I am the damned flight
  of the mad moth,
    dancing halos around the flame.
I am the moon call
  of the lone wolf,
    strolling bloodied across the
        plains.
I am the disease that gives to death;
  the cold hand
    that receives the wilted corpse.

The warm breath
    that sends it back.

I start the storms with my breath.
    Flood the lands when I feel like it.
In some places,
    I set a fire.
In others,
    I knock coconuts from the tree
        into cool blue waters.

Dare not try to fathom me;
    insanity looks wise,
        next to
    my ways.

VERSE X

I am the whore
    and the one who frequents her
              bed.
I am the bride
    and the one she chooses to wed.
I am the piles of gold kings hoard.
    I am the rags that cover beggar's
              loins.
I am the gods who tell men how to
              live.
    I am the demons who destroy
              best-laid plans.
I lead adulterers toward flesh,
    by their deviant hands.

I stride toward shadows.
    Laugh in the darkness.
Dance deathless
    upon my own grave.
And I live not between two certain
              oblivions,
    but outside of them.

For the web of the world does not
              deceive me.

The smoke of delusion will never
blind me.
When you feed me poison
—I lick the plate!

You always thought I was up there,
down there,
or over there.
You always thought I was in here,
made there,
or just unaware.

Friend,
when did you forget
you are
The One—
you are looking for?

I steal the last breath from the dying.
   I pull the babe from the womb.
I decide on the length of lives.
   I am to blame for death,
     and to thank for life.

I fall to the ground from my own
               branch tips.
   Rear my head toward my own
               feet.
I grow up at my own side,
   then steal the sun from myself
     and lend myself the shade.
When I die,
   I make a meal
     of my mind.

I am the designer of destiny,
   and destiny herself.
I am the beginning,
   the middle,
     the end.

Small things are great to me.
   Great things are small to me.
The thousand tongues of the earth

speak the same language as me.
All appearances are good to me.
No word in the air
   that I did not first utter,
      or allow to be.

Truly,
   my friend,
      all this is my name.

Yet, like the evanescence of the sky,
   this self-sublime,

      I can but explain—

VERSE XII

I beat your heart,
  from morning through night.
I shut your eyes,
  pry them open again.
Your blood spills from my cup.
  Your mind beholds my vision.

When the wind blows,
  you inhale my breath.
When the rain falls,
  you taste my tears.
When the sun shines,
  you embrace my arms.
When you fall asleep
  —I watch over myself.

Know in ignorance,
  you claim to be man.
Matured by wisdom,
  you will declare your illusion.
Awakened by truth,
  you shall realize
    my absolute conclusion—

I am the supreme Self,
  at the center of all selves.

I am the supernal Soul,
   among all souls.
Unity and duality measure nothing
       to me.
  I am above distinctions;
    I belong here.

My name is Insane;
  my sole friend,
    my mad self.

  —She who is forever to blame.

VERSE XIII

When night falls in my country,
    I perceive no darkness.
When day breaks in my country,
    I discern no difference.
In my summer no heat rises;
    in my winter no cold freezes.
My tides do not turn;
    my mountains do not crumble.

For I am
    the one long day.
        "The one—long—day!"
And I never end.
    And closer still,
        I never began.

So when old brother fate rolls in,
    I toss my gold in the air.
Of where it lands,
    and into whose hands,
        I am utterly free from care.

Know in my pocket lies the book
    that notes the end of all ages.
Come close,
    and I shall reveal to you

the glorious
 —empty pages.

My sonnet for life overwhelms.
 There are no shores to my seas,
  nor ends to my realms.

I see no evil,
 hear no evil,
  speak no evil.
I see no good,
 hear no good,
  speak no good.

I am like mad honey.
 Sweet!
  And lethal

 to all the senses—

PART THREE

I dance to mad tunes;
   I am lord of the pleasure domes.
I drink from candlelight to sunlight.
I wear my life on my sleeve;
   I hang my coat where I please.
I am the liberal one,
   who wears royal qualities.
I am wild
   beyond belief!

Often joyous,
   rarely sad.
Sometimes kind,
   always mad.
Fascinated, disinterested,
   and astray.
Loyal, loving,
   and sublimely ordinary.

I orient by disorientation.
   I disorient by orientation.
I steal the stones from the vanishing
          path,
   then cast them into the ocean.
Yet, when the tides pull these things
          away,

my inner smile never falters.
And though I may welcome you to
   walk straight over me

     —I am untouchable.

I am the signature of all things.
   I am the bronze axle
     upon which the cosmos spins.
I am nothing forever,
   and ever,
     and ever.

I am beyond,
   Beyond.

Perfect,
   formless,
     taintless

   —wilderness.

VERSE XV

I am the actor,
   the stage,
      and the audience.
I am the playwright,
   the lines,
      and the story.
This is how my show works.
   Knowing this,
      which part do you play?

I am the masquerade party,
   the ballroom,
      and the guests.
I am the host,
   the music,
      and the masks.
This is how my show works.
   Knowing this,
      how can you be invited?

For I am the spectator,
   and the spectated.
I am the witness,
   and the witnessed.
When I am rich,
   I play richness.

When I am poor,
   I play poverty.
When I am drunk,
   I play drunkenness.
When I am passionate,
   I play passionately.

Then, as the reveler joins the parade,
   I join the world and

      —*sing surreal!*

Yet, with the animals in the dark,
   I am honest.
I lay my forehead
   softly upon their own,
      and say nothing—

VERSE XVI

You who do not hold a view,
   behold me.
You who do not mention an opinion,
   speak of me.
Those who live unbiasedly,
   embrace me.
The large and small
   measure up to me.

You will not spot me in a crowd.
   I will not raise my hand when
           called.
When you ask for my real name,
   I will utter whatever is suitable.

Among the shadows,
   I fail to hide my light.
Under the light,
   I never fail to show my shadows.
Hopelessly honest,
   I am a contradiction to all
     but myself.

For I am unborn and unmade.
   I am mystery and metamorphosis.
I am the beautiful and the beloved.

I am the outcast and despised.
I blast misfortune,
   emptiness,
     and despair
   in my furnace
     —then toss them by the
              wayside.

So let all judgments fall upon me.
   My nature is not defiled
     by the words of the world,
   and could not care less for them.

Life and Death are good
   —I like them.

Yet they come nowhere close
   to the rich-tasting splendor
     —of my truth.

VERSE XVII

The mountains
   are my splendid young children.
I allow them to play in my garden
   a million, million years.
With the caress of my palm,
   I grind them to dust.
With my breath,
   I shall build them once again.
In this way,
   the confused call me the father.

The sky
   is my divine breast.
The universe suckles the air from it,
   as I hold its head.
I look at my baby
   before I whisper in its ear,
     "One day, my darling, you shall
           die."
Then, smiling,
   I adjust myself,
     and feed it more life.
In this way,
   the confused call me the mother.

Truly, though,
    I have no son or daughter.
I was born of no mother,
    I was raised by no father.
       I have neither a brother
              nor a sister.
I orphaned yours truly,
    at the beginning of time.

My family is

    —Myself.

VERSE XVIII

When chaos reigns,
   I run the streets with the knaves.
When the storm blows in,
   I swing open my hatches.
When the sea floods my shore,
   I gleefully grab my old gold cup.
You can shoot me down on the street
   —I will get up!

My essence is theft-proof.
   My walls are unscalable.
On the shores of my great moat
   lie a thousand torn shipwrecks.

Death cannot catch me.
   Diseases dare not enter me.
     Madness knows not to devour
         me.
For I am free,
   and always in good health.

VERSE XIX

I hold a knife to Intellect's throat.
  Emotions watch my murderous
            step.
They are my welcome guests,
  and I enjoy their company.
When they get drunk,
  I cast them out.

I do not suffer seriousness.
  My mind is ever intoxicated
      with supreme bliss.
When a fool interferes with my
            games,
  I strike him with my stick.
Then, cursing,
  I throw my boot after him.

Flawless is my footing.
  Absent is my suffering.
When the world turns upside down

  —I admire the view!

VERSE XX

My country has no borders.
   My kingdom rules without laws.
There are no peasants outside my
              gates,
   and no treasure in my towers.
I am equal; inside
   —and out.

I am naturally supernatural.
   My heart combusts spontaneously.
I am the Soul of all souls.
   I am the Heart of all hearts.
     I am the Mind of all minds.
   I am the Thought
     behind all thoughts.

I am the author of worlds seen
   and unseen.
I hide universes from one another
   by tucking them inside each other.
Look to your left,
   you may just catch one flicker.

   —Who cares!

In the one wild wilderness,

I am the only living beast.
And I need no faith
   to run blind
      through my silver woods at
               night.

For I am
   in between
      all things.
And all things are
   in between me.
Tell me, friend,
   who can stop my tracks?

This vision perfect.
   This voice divine.
When I wake up,
   virgins enter my chamber,
      then pour me fine wine.

Know, alone I sit,
   and dream this life

      —*to Life.*

PART FOUR

VERSE XXI

To whom should I offer prayers,
   or fetter my oblations?
Which limb of mine
   may claim providence over the
             other?
Dedications are vanity.
   Salutations are insanity.
Did I ever shut truth out
   in the name of an altar?
My old madness was never shy!

When is the right time to worship
           me?
   Dusk, night, or day?
Which hour may I read holy books
    by candlelight?
I am the prayer;
   I wrote the books.
My candle is the sun,
   and I shall blow it out
     when the whim takes me.

Tear down my images,
   erase my name from your tongue.
If you ever built a wall around me,
   knock it to the ground.

I am uncontainable,
   uncontaminated,
      unpronounceable.

So lay down your alms bowls,
   throw away your
      little sacred spiritual things.
Make love to me,
   without your veil.
In the morning,
   I will still be here.

I love you
   —I made You.

VERSE XXII

I am the end of all beginnings
   and the beginning of all ends.
I am the hate of those who hate me.
I am the love of those who love me.
I am the doubt of those who
              doubt me.
I am the violence of those who
              violate me.
I am the splendor of those who
              know me.
I am the ignorance of those who
              have never heard of me.
I am the teacher of comprehending.
I am the fool who misunderstands.

I am the sun,
   the stars,
      the moon—

I am the all
   you can hold in your hands.

VERSE XXIII

I tilt my head,
    watch all roads lead to me.
I roll my cuffs,
    let all rivers flow into me.

Old Man North
    extends his hand.
Lady South
    thanks me for her holy,
      holy land.
East and West
    each offer a desert rose.
How I made this kingdom
    is unimaginable to show.

The blind arrive,
    then leave with eyes.
The seers arrive,
    then leave blinded.
Crazed is she
    who dares climb aboard
      my crystal carriage.

Risking it all
    to leave
      mindless—

VERSE XXIV

When your senses stray,
   you haul them in.
When your thoughts run away,
   you throw on the cuffs.
Know I have none of these
             afflictions.

When I close my eyes,
   the world appears!
When I open my eyes,
   illusion disappears!

For I do not know myself with
          myself.
   Nor do I understand or fathom my
          meaning.
I am the middle of the universe.
   Yet when I go there,
     I am missing?
Still this makes perfect sense to me
   —I am pure being!

So I dress in fur gowns,
   and wear gold crowns,
     then wander my home
          unbounded.

When I feel like it,
   I get so drunk
      I steal flowers from my own
             garden.

Know in my old delusion
   I found this world unfair,

    —now it is not even there.

VERSE XXV

I am disillusioned from this place.
Nothing does not scare me.
    Death blushes when he sees me.
When I walk in the temple,
    saints march out.
When I bathe in unholy waters,
    snakes jump out!

I am incorruptible.
    —I am not here.

I was a proud porcelain pot till
    Truth broke me.
I was a delicate glass flute till
    Reality played me.
I was a careful earthen vase till
    Existence dropped me.

Death to the world
    and her sorrows!
I am the mind unfettered.
    I am the twice-born newborn.
Lock me up,
    throw away the key.

A slave to the rhythm

—I shall always break free!

Unreality
    has nothing
        on me.

VERSE XXVI

Strange to you,
  yet not a stranger.
Familiar to you,
  yet not an acquaintance.
Unexpected to you,
  but not unannounced.
I arrive at your deepest invitation
  —this is my house.

As whales swim beneath the waves,
  all is contained by me.
As swallows soar through the sky,
  all is held by me.
Yet, try to speak to the whales of the
        sea,
  or the swallows of the sky,
    and they shall know nothing of
        me.

I am indivisible
  and invisible—
    clear and plain as day.
I am visible
  and immutable—
    carefully hidden behind a
  secret, *secret*.

I am the eye that never shuts.
   I watch illusion
      and reality
   dance each night and day.

I am this song that never ends.
   And I sing my one long swan song,
      upon my own ears,
   never ceasing

     —ever endlessly.

When the world is not here
  —I am.
When illusion has gone
  —I remain.
When unreality wakes up to
       congratulate me
  —I run away.

I am beyond the real
  and the unreal.
Beyond the holy
  and the unholy.
Truth
  and untruth.
Here
  and there.

All the world is asleep to me,
  yet I am the only one at rest.
All the world is deaf and dumb to
      me,
  yet I am the only one who knows
      silence.

And I curse the words
  of the blessed who find me.

And condemn them
    from the proud singing tree
        to the old silent cage.

My truth silences me.
    All words fail me.

Even this honest song

    —was a grand lie.

PART FIVE

VERSE XXVIII

Tell me, friend—
    where did you seek
        to go in this world?
And what did you dream
    lay at the end
        of all those many roads?
Did you truly believe
    you would find it,
        and pick a rose from its secret
                garden?

Did you never suspect,
    just once,
        the destination for which
                you lived
    did not exist?
And those who cheat death
    by one hundred years
        barely reach my first breath.

So let go of your rusted rail
    and learn to love this storm.
The body is the vessel
    that stops you merging back into
                me.
The mind is the anchor

tethering you
    to the shores of this world.
So pray furiously,
    that a great wind may thrash your
                    sail,
        and wash you back
    upon my shoreless shore.

Then, understanding this,
    on quiet days
        where the lovely sun shines
    and the songbirds sing,
        you shall soon
    grow jealous of

        —the dead.

VERSE XXIX

The morning arrives,
   the dew evaporates from the
         leaves.
    Why complicate things?
The night falls,
   the moon waxes.
    Could life be any simpler?
I take a long sleep,
   the world begins.
    Why trouble over a storm in a
         thimble?

There are no trespassers in my fields
   to tie down my heart.
I carry no sword or shield.
Like the little brook,
   I skip swearless
     over the fallen oak
   back toward my ocean.

At dusk,
   on fishing boats in the harbor,
     I lie around
   and pour my many selves wine.
Then, at midnight,
   I visit this world,

and wander from room to
room.

I watch fools fight
  and the wise make love.
In other places,
  people pray I grant them
    what they already have.

Smiling,
  I throw on my splendid coat,
    and leave them all to it—

Be illuminated!
  Watch the stars.
    —They know the truth.
Be playful!
  Watch the children.
    —They know the truth.
Be simple!
  Watch the trees.
    —They know the truth.
Be gentle!
  Watch the lambs.
    —They know the truth.
Be still!
  Watch the dead.
    —They know
  the truth.

Your world is the cart,
  and I am the cart driver.
Your body is the pot,
  and I am the pot maker.
Your blood is red wine,
  and I am the winemaker.
Your thoughts are gray clouds,
  and I am the rainmaker.
Your words are my breath,

and I am
  the breath—
taker.

You are the dream,
  I am
    —the Dream Maker.

OUTRO

When illusion and reality
   are strange shapes
      that melt in your thoughts.

When you are at once the altar,
   the pilgrim who circles it,
      and the prayer he offers.

When your vision is immovable
   and illuminable,
      yet completely blind
   to all creation.

When alpha devours omega,
   infinity becomes finite,
      and eternity draws to
   "The End."

When there is nothing left
   that is holy,
      and nothing that is not.

When there is no day
   nor night to be spoken of,
      and time has been put away.

When nightmares and dreamscapes
   have woken up
      to their own extinction.

When intelligence and emotion
   and knowledge and wisdom
      have all understood the
                  completeness
   of absolutely nothing.

When selflessness is absurd,
   charity shameless,
      and detachment insane.

When you are no longer home,
   heading there,
      or lost.

When there is no more north
   to guide you forward,
      or south
   to ground your feet.

When the seeker
   becomes the sought,
      and the made
   becomes the maker.

When the door through which

you long sought to pass
   lies already closed behind.

When the path is no longer a path,
   but a constant arriving.

When "The Good Fight,"
   "The Journey,"
      and "The Way"
   all prove to be elaborate detours.

When you have never been born,
   let alone could possibly die.

When your dwellings are free
   from interior and exterior.

When there is no bondage
   to be free of
      and no freedom
   to speak of.

When you can no longer renounce,
   or possess,
      a single atom.

When you have devoured
   your own tail,
      and found nothing left over.

When beginnings,
  middles,
    and ends
  are one moment that never
            happened.

When not a single good deed
  has ever been done,
    nor a single sin
  ever begun.

When you are anchored
  so deep beneath,
    there is no coming or going.

When time has orphaned you,
  and no past, present, or future
    exist to belong to.

When your palms, the sky,
  the birds, your lovers,
    the warm earth beneath your
            feet
  are not,
    and never were.

And finally,
  when you understand

you shall never arrive,
and all honorable quests
were made in vain.

You shall ultimately see,
    when you touch the sun
        —only I remain.

Then,
    like a queen wears her robe,
        you shall wear this all.

Erotic to the bone,
    now crowned
        The One
    who has destroyed the world.

Those that know you
    shall name you
        "Sky-clad."

Then of what more should I sing,
    but this primordial uni-*verse*.

My precious
    song of the soul,

    THE HYMN—

IVVIIMMIX

Read & share for free:

Lightning Source UK Ltd.
Milton Keynes UK
UKHW011125161219
355473UK00001B/2/P